20 Questions: Earth Science

What Do You Know About

Plate Tectonics?

Gillian Gosman

PowerKiDS
press™

New York

Published in 2014 by The Rosen Publishing Group, Inc.
29 East 21st Street, New York, NY 10010

Copyright © 2014 by The Rosen Publishing Group, Inc.

First Edition

Editor: Jennifer Way
Book Design: Kate Laczynski
Layout Design: Andrew Povolny

Gosman, Gillian.
What do you know about plate tectonics? / by Gillian Gosman. — 1st ed.
    p. cm. — (20 questions: Earth science)
Includes index.
ISBN 978-1-4488-9698-1 (library binding) — ISBN 978-1-4488-9854-1 (pbk.) —
ISBN 978-1-4488-9855-8 (6-pack)
1. Plate tectonics—Juvenile literature. I. Title.
QE511.4.G67 2013
551.1'36—dc23

                                                                        2012030674

Manufactured in the United States of America

CPSIA Compliance Information: Batch #S13PK5: For Further Information contact Rosen Publishing, New York, New York at 1-800-237-9932

Contents

What Do You Know About Plate Tectonics?

The ground beneath you feels like it is standing still, right? Well, it is not! It moves very slowly, but over time that movement has changed the way that Earth looks. Millions of years from now, Earth will look much different from the way it does today. **Plate tectonics** is the study of this movement.

In this book, we will learn about the layers of Earth and how Earth's plates move over time and reshape continents and other landforms. You will also learn about the sometimes dangerous results of all this change as well as the science behind our understanding of Earth's transformation.

It may not seem like they change, but mountains do change slowly over time, just like the rest of Earth's crust.

1. What are Earth's layers?

Earth is made up of four main layers. At the center is the core. The inner core is a solid ball of metals. The outer core is liquid metal. The next layer is the mantle, which can be divided into the mantle and the upper mantle. The mantle is made up of solid rock, but the upper part of the mantle gets so hot that the rock melts and moves. The top layer is the crust. It is made of many different kinds of rocks.

Here is lava spreading along the ground. As it cools, it hardens into rock.

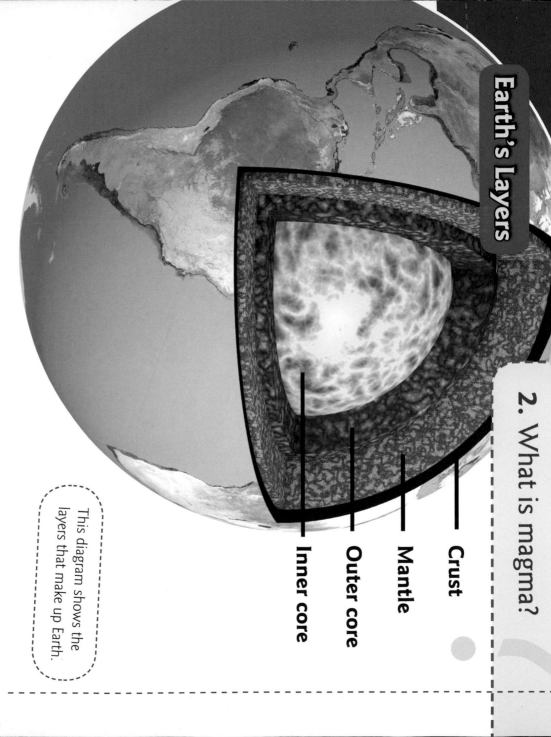

This diagram shows the layers that make up Earth.

Inner core

Outer core

Mantle

Crust

2. What is magma?

Magma is molten, or melted, rock under Earth's crust. When magma erupts through Earth's crust, the melted rock is called **lava**.

7

3. How thick are Earth's layers?

Together, the inner core and outer core are about 2,000 miles (3,219 km) thick. The mantle is roughly 1,700 miles (2,735 km) thick. The crust and the upper mantle are only about 37 miles (60 km) thick in most places. The crust is thinner underneath the ocean and thicker where there are mountains.

Have you ever dug a hole in the ground? You were digging into Earth's crust.

8

Earth's crust is made up of pieces called plates. The seven largest plates are called the African, North American, South American, Eurasian, Indian-Australian, Antarctic, and Pacific plates. There are other smaller plates, such as the Nazca and Arabian plates. These plates are on the move, sliding across Earth's surface at about the same speed at which your fingernails grow.

Earth's Plates

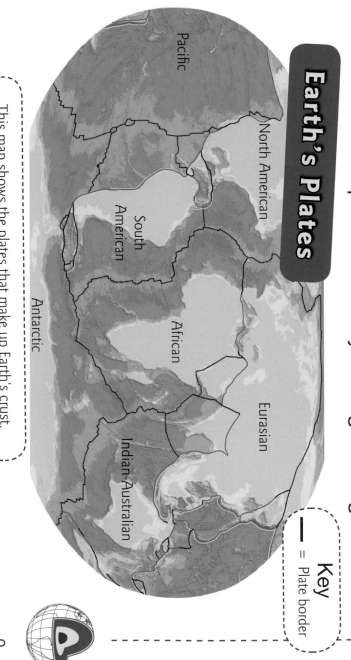

Pacific

North American

South American

Antarctic

African

Eurasian

Indian-Australian

Key
— = Plate border

This map shows the plates that make up Earth's crust.

5. What is continental drift?

Continental drift is a **theory** created by a scientist named Alfred Wegener in 1912. He believed that the continents had not always been in their present locations. This theory inspired many other scientists to study continental movement. The theory of continental drift was later replaced by the theory of plate tectonics.

6. How do the plates move?

The hardened, cool plates of the crust slide over the thick, partially melted rock of the upper mantle.

Plates move between 1 and 10 inches (2.5–25 cm) each year. Over time, this movement adds up. About 300 million years ago, the plates formed a **supercontinent** called Pangaea. Over time, the plates moved apart and formed the seven continents we know today.

Pangaea

Today's Earth

The map on the left shows the supercontinent Pangaea. Scientists think that it began to break up about 200 million years ago. The map on the right shows how the continents look today. Notice that you can see how the continents once fit together.

8. What is divergence?

When the continental plates move apart, this movement is called **divergence**, or spreading.

This cutaway diagram shows what the rifts and ridges under the ocean look like.

Ocean Ridges and Rifts

Ocean ridge

Ocean rift

Oceanic crust

Crust and part of upper mantle

Upper mantle

Plates often break apart along two **parallel** lines, leaving a strip of crust between them. This piece of crust sinks, forming a rift. Magma from below Earth's surface rises to fill the cracks, hardens, and forms new crust.

The Rio Grande Rift is a continental rift that extends from Colorado to Mexico. The river called the Rio Grande runs through the rift. In the Atlantic Ocean, an underwater rift runs alongside the Mid-Atlantic Ridge. This is an underwater mountain range that runs nearly the entire length of the planet!

The Rio Grande, shown here, runs through a continental rift.

10. What is convergence?

Convergence is the coming together of plates. As the plates come together, they will either be pushed above the crust's surface, forming mountains, or pushed down below the crust's surface, forming trenches.

The Himalayas formed through the convergence between the Indian-Australian plate and the Eurasian plate.

Mountains are formed when the plates converge and are pushed up. The plates then fold and form mountains. The Andes, in South America, the Rocky Mountains, in North America, the Alps, in Europe, and the Himalayas, in Asia, all formed in this way.

12. What is subduction?

Subduction is what happens when plates meet and one plate slides below the other. The lower plate sinks into the mantle, and some of the rock becomes molten.

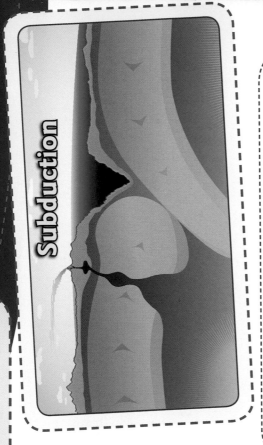

Subduction

This picture shows a subduction zone, where one plate (right) is sliding below the other (left). A piece of the lower plate is melting and causing a volcano to form on the upper plate.

13. How do plates form ocean trenches?

Trenches are formed when the front end of one plate slides below the front end of another plate. Trenches are most common when an ocean plate slides under the continental plate, creating a deep underwater trench.

Volcanoes can form in several ways. In areas of subduction, the lower plate can melt, causing cracks to form in the upper plate, which allow magma to erupt. Rifts also can cause volcanoes when they create cracks that allow magma to reach Earth's surface. This means that volcanoes can form in both areas of convergence and divergence.

Volcano

15. What are transform boundaries?

When plates slide alongside each other in opposite directions, the line where they meet is called a **transform boundary**. Long, rocky valleys may form where the two plates grind past each other.

The Vasquez Rocks, in California, were formed by the action along the San Andreas fault.

The break in Earth's crust caused by the movements of plates in a transform boundary is known as a **fault** line or fault zone. The most famous fault zone in the United States is the San Andreas fault, in California.

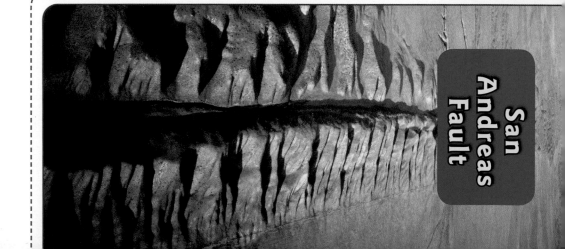

San Andreas Fault

17. What are slips?

A slip describes how the plates along a fault line move in relation to one another. When the higher plate moves down and the lower plate moves up, the fault line is called a dip slip. When the two pieces move past each other, the fault line is called a strike slip.

18. How do plates cause earthquakes?

Earthquakes can happen wherever plates converge, diverge, or move past one another. The movement of plates is not smooth and easy. The plates grind against each other, breaking down rocks and locking together. When the edge of one plate catches the edge of the other and the two plates lock together, pressure builds up. When they finally break loose, the sudden movement is felt as an earthquake.

The earthquake that hit Haiti in 2010 was one of the deadliest and most destructive earthquakes in history.

Alfred Wegener's theory of continental drift did not explain why or how the continents moved. Scientists began to look for an explanation. They studied the **magnetic** features of Earth's crust, especially on the ocean floor. By the mid-1960s, they had an understanding of how plate tectonics worked.

Here a scientist is looking at a seismometer. This is an instrument that allows scientists to measure and locate earthquakes and volcanic activity.

21

20. What do rocks and fossils tell us about plate tectonics?

Looking at rocks and **fossils** shows you how plate tectonics have shaped our planet. For example, the same types of rocks are often found on continents on opposite sides of oceans. In addition, fossils of similar plant and animal **species** are also often found on continents that today are separated by oceans. This evidence suggests that Earth's continents have moved over time. By studying rocks, fossils, earthquakes, and volcanoes, scientists who study plate tectonics try to guess how Earth will continue to change.

Fossils, like the one shown here, give scientists clues about Earth's history, including the history of the movement of Earth's plates.

22

Glossary

convergence (kun-VER-jents) The coming together of plates.

divergence (duh-VER-jents) When continental plates move apart.

fault (FAWLT) A crack in Earth's crust, or outside.

fossils (FO-sulz) The hardened remains of dead animals or plants.

lava (LAH-vuh) Hot, melted rock that comes out of a volcano.

magma (MAG-muh) Hot, melted rock inside Earth.

magnetic (mag-NEH-tik) Having to do with the force that pulls certain objects toward one another.

parallel (PAR-uh-lel) Being the same distance apart at all points.

plate tectonics (PLAYT tek-TAH-niks) The study of the moving pieces of Earth's crust.

species (SPEE-sheez) One kind of living thing. All people are one species.

subduction (sub-DUK-shun) What happens when two plates hit and one forces the other into Earth's mantle.

supercontinent (SOO-per-kon-tuh-nent) A huge landmass made up of several of today's continents.

theory (THEE-uh-ree) An idea or group of ideas that tries to explain something.

transform boundary (tranz-FORM BOWN-duh-ree) The line where plates that are sliding alongside each other meet.

Index

C
convergence, 14, 17
core, 6, 8
crust, 6–10, 13,
  19, 21

D
divergence, 12, 17

E
Earth, 4, 6, 22

L
landforms, 4

lava, 7
layer(s), 4, 6

M
magma 7, 13, 17
mantle, 6, 8, 10, 16
mountains, 6, 8,
  14–15

O
ocean(s), 8, 13, 22

P
piece(s), 9, 13, 19

plate(s), 4, 9–20

R
results, 4

S
species, 22
subduction, 16–17
supercontinent, 11

T
theory, 10, 21
transform boundary,
  18–19

Websites

Due to the changing nature of Internet links, PowerKids Press has developed an online list of websites related to the subject of this book. This site is updated regularly. Please use this link to access the list:
www.powerkidslinks.com/20es/plate/

24